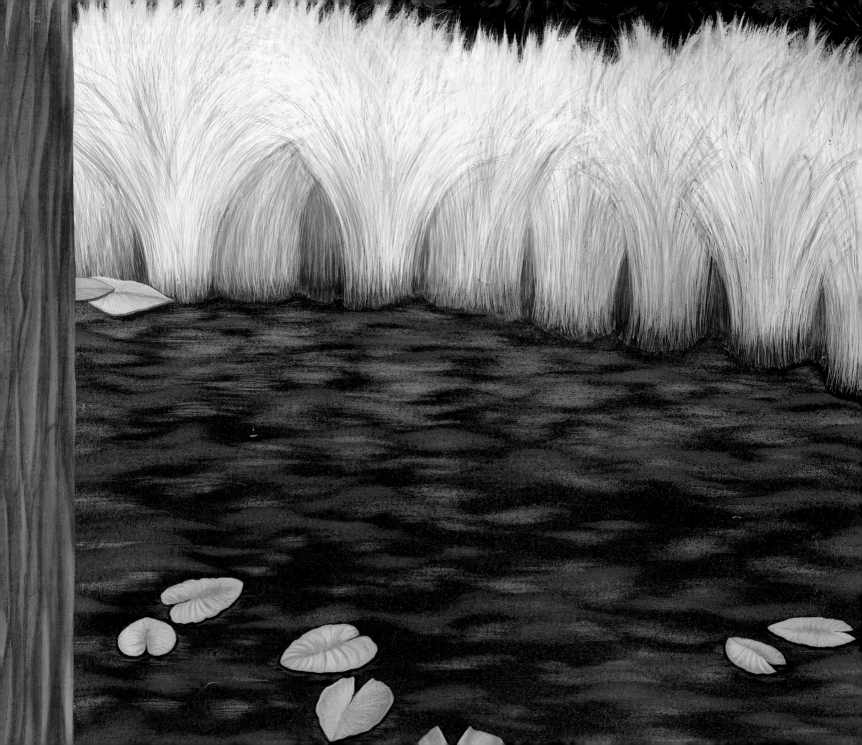

Beaver at Long Pond

by **William T. George** and **Lindsay Barrett George**

pictures by **Lindsay Barrett George**

 Greenwillow Books, New York

Library of Congress Cataloging-in-Publication Data
George, William T.   Beaver at Long Pond.
Summary: As the other animals at Long Pond settle
down for the night, Beaver leaves his lodge, begins
searching for food, and starts his nightly adventure.
1. Beavers—Juvenile literature.   [1. Beavers]
I. George, Lindsay Barrett.   II. Title.
QL737.R632G46 1988   599.23'32   87-281
ISBN 0-688-07106-6   ISBN 0-688-07107-4 (lib. bdg.)

FOR
AUNT
PEGGY

It is dusk at Long Pond. Most of the animals
have settled down for the night—the birds in the
trees, the wood ducks in the tall grasses, and
the painted turtles at the bottom of the pond.

The beaver opens
his eyes. It is time
to search for food.
He swims out of his lodge
through the underwater tunnel.
He looks up through the water
to the sky, but it is still too
light to go on shore.
Instead, he finds some water lily
roots and eats them.

The beaver swims to the surface and sees the first star in the sky. He circles the pond, sniffing for danger. As he nears the outlet of the pond, he feels a pull on his whiskers. He stops swimming. He hears the sound of rushing water. There is a break in the dam! He is frightened and sniffs the wind, but smells no danger.

The beaver cuts some blueberry
branches with his teeth. He carries
the branches to the break in the
dam and pushes mud against
them with his head.

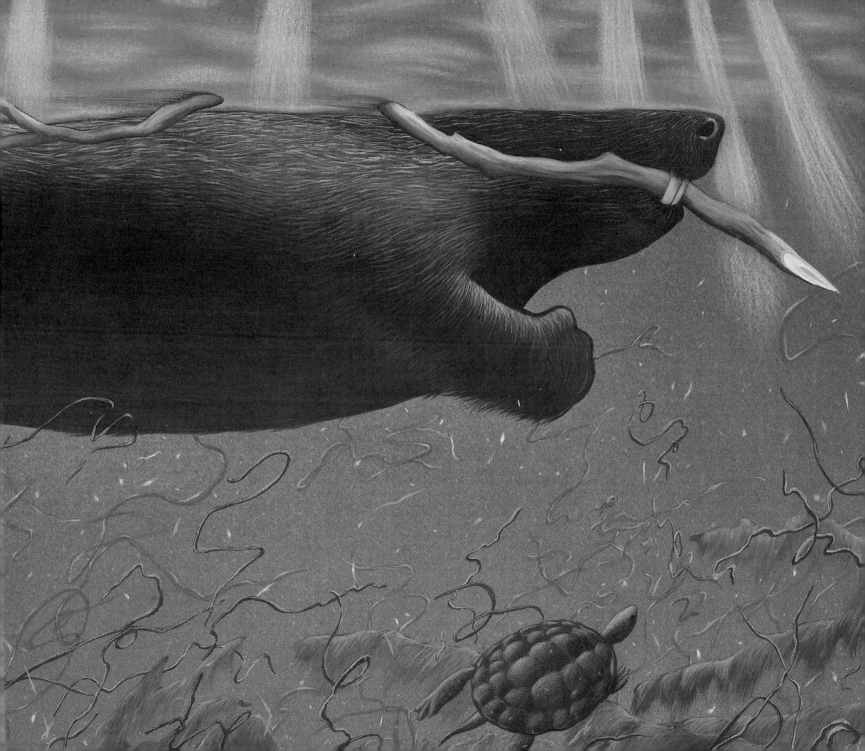

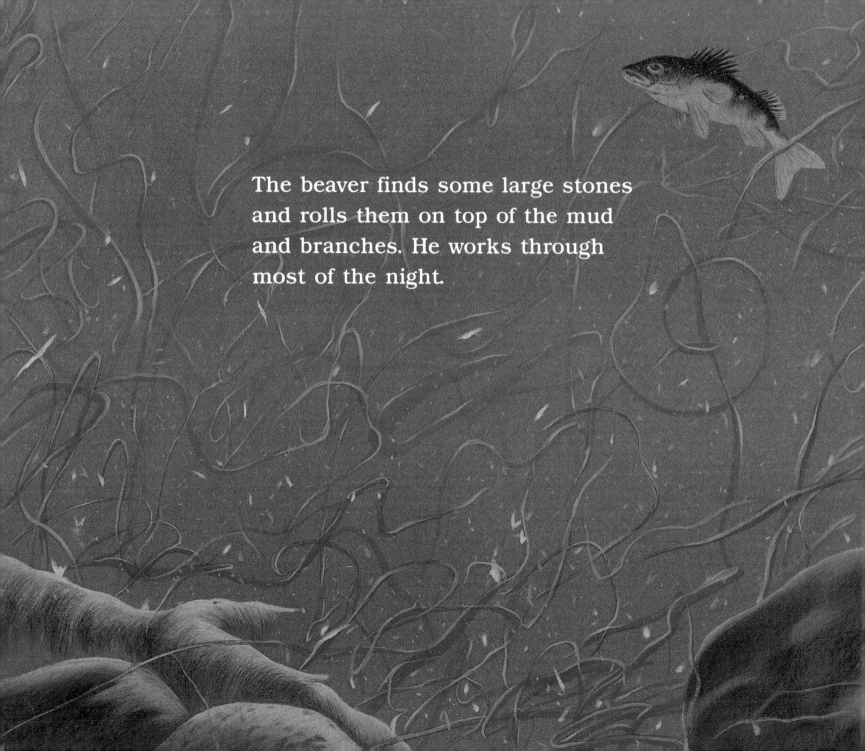

The beaver finds some large stones
and rolls them on top of the mud
and branches. He works through
most of the night.

The moon is high in the sky. The beaver swims into the wind, sniffing constantly. He reaches the shore, knowing it is safe, and begins the search for food. He passes up maple trees, oaks, and pines. At last he comes to a grove of black birch trees.

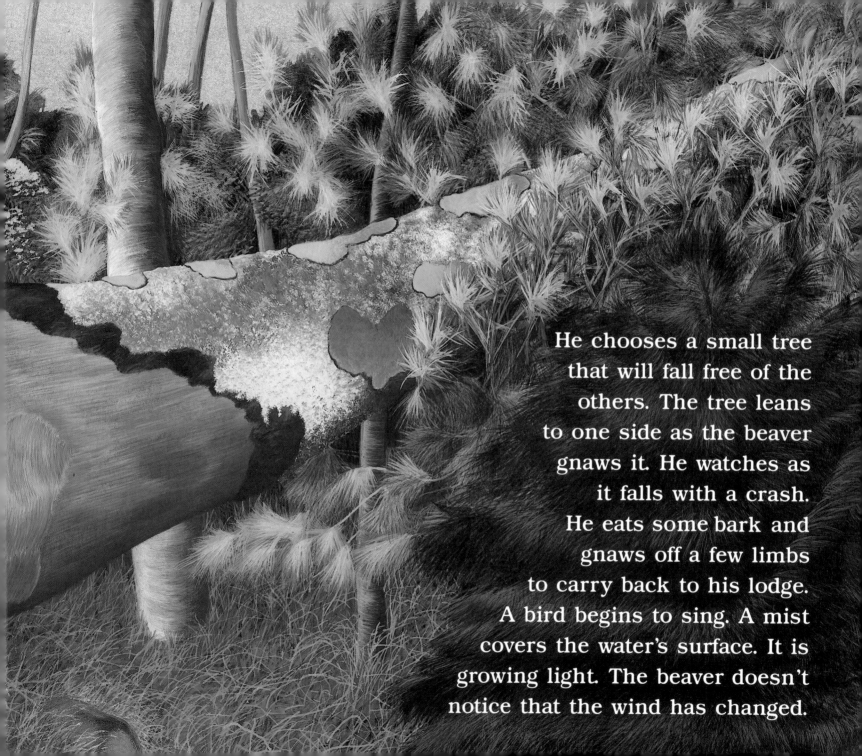

He chooses a small tree that will fall free of the others. The tree leans to one side as the beaver gnaws it. He watches as it falls with a crash. He eats some bark and gnaws off a few limbs to carry back to his lodge. A bird begins to sing. A mist covers the water's surface. It is growing light. The beaver doesn't notice that the wind has changed.

A boy and his dog are walking toward the pond. They are going fishing. The beaver is chewing noisily on the black birch tree. What is that strange sound, the boy wonders, as he nears the pond. Suddenly they are face-to-face.

No one moves. The beaver gnashes his teeth.
The dog barks and charges. The beaver scurries
down to the pond. He reaches it just in time,
slaps the water with his great tail, and dives to
safety. The dog stands barking at the water.

The beaver surfaces in the middle of the pond.
He looks back and sees the dog and the boy
standing on the shore.
He is safe, and it is time to go home.

The wood ducks have left the tall grasses to search for food. The turtles have swum to the edge of the pond, looking for insects. The beaver circles his lodge one last time, sniffing for trouble. All is safe.

He dives down and swims
through the tunnel to his lodge.
He grooms his fur. His eyes close.
The beaver sleeps.
It has been a long night.